MW01206249

A GRATITUDE JOURNAL

THIS JOURNAL BELONGS TO:

....

....

A **OWN** notebooks PRODUCTION

Date: .... Day: ....

Today I am Grateful for

....

....

....

....

....

....

The art of life is to know
how to enjoy a little and
to endure very much.

-William Hazlitt

1

Date:........................... Day:...............................

Today I am Grateful for

....

....

....

....

....

Date:........................... Day:...............................

Today I am Grateful for

....

....

....

....

....

When you go in search
of honey you must expect
to be stung by bees.
-Joseph Joubert

Date: .... Day: ....

Today I am Grateful for

....

....

....

....

....

....

Date:........................ Day:..............................

Today I am Grateful for

....
....
....
....
....
....

Date:........................ Day:..............................

Today I am Grateful for

....
....
....
....
....

Date: .... Day: ....

Today I am Grateful for

....

....

....

....

....

....

Happiness resides not in possessions, and not in gold, happiness dwells in the soul.

-Democritus

Date: .... Day: ....

Today I am Grateful for

....

....

....

....

....

....

Date: .... Day: ....

Today I am Grateful for

....

....

....

....

....

....

If you think you can win,
you can win. Faith is
necessary to victory.
-*William Hazlitt*

Date: .... Day: ....

Today I am Grateful for

....

....

....

....

....

....

Date:.......................... Day:..............................

Today I am Grateful for

....

....

....

....

....

Date:.......................... Day:..............................

Today I am Grateful for

....

....

....

....

....

Date: .... Day: ....

Today I am Grateful for

....

....

....

....

....

....

The aim of argument,
or of discussion, should
not be victory, but
progress.

-Joseph Joubert

Date:_____ Day:_____

Today I am Grateful for

....
....
....
....
....
....

Date:_____ Day:_____

Today I am Grateful for

....
....
....
....
....
....

Date: .... Day: ....

Today I am Grateful for

....

....

....

....

....

....

Thoughts without
content are empty,
intuitions without
concepts are blind.
-Immanuel Kant

Date: .... Day: ....

Today I am Grateful for

....

....

....

....

....

Date: .... Day: ....

Today I am Grateful for

....

....

....

....

....

There is no friendship, no love, like that of the parent for the child.
-Henry Ward Beecher

Date: .... Day: ....

Today I am Grateful for

....

....

....

....

....

....

Date: .... Day: ....

Today I am Grateful for

....

....

....

....

....

Date: .... Day: ....

Today I am Grateful for

....

....

....

....

....

Date: _____ Day: _____

Today I am Grateful for

....

....

....

....

....

....

Our sins are more easily
remembered than our
good deeds.

-Democritus

Date: .... Day: ....

Today I am Grateful for

....

....

....

....

....

....

Date: .... Day: ....

Today I am Grateful for

....

....

....

....

....

Books are the treasured wealth of the world and the fit inheritance of generations and nations.
-Henry David Thoreau

Date: .... Day: ....

Today I am Grateful for

....

....

....

....

....

....

Date: .... Day: ....

Today I am Grateful for

....

....

....

....

....

....

Date: .... Day: ....

Today I am Grateful for

....

....

....

....

....

Date: _____ Day: _____

Today I am Grateful for

....

....

....

....

....

The more we do,
the more we can do.
-William Hazlitt

Date: .... Day: ....

Today I am Grateful for

....

....

....

....

....

Date: .... Day: ....

Today I am Grateful for

....

....

....

....

....

Date: _____ Day: _____

Today I am Grateful for

....

....

....

....

....

....

Kindness is loving people more than they deserve.
-Joseph Joubert

Date:................................ Day:....................................

Today I am Grateful for

....

....

....

....

....

....

Date:................................ Day:....................................

Today I am Grateful for

....

....

....

....

....

Education is an ornament
for the prosperous,
a refuge for the
unfortunate.

-Democritus

Date: .... Day: ....

Today I am Grateful for

....

....

....

....

....

....

23

Date:................................ Day:...

Today I am Grateful for

....

....

....

....

....

Date:................................ Day:...

Today I am Grateful for

....

....

....

....

....

Date: .... Day: ....

Today I am Grateful for

....

....

....

....

....

No truly great
person ever thought
themselves so.

-William Hazlitt

Date: .... Day: ....

Today I am Grateful for

....

....

....

....

....

Date: .... Day: ....

Today I am Grateful for

....

....

....

....

....

It's easier to go down
a hill than up it but the
view is much better
at the top.

-Henry Ward Beecher

Date: _____ Day: _____

Today I am Grateful for

_____

_____

_____

_____

_____

Date: .... Day: ....

Today I am Grateful for

....

....

....

....

....

....

Date: .... Day: ....

Today I am Grateful for

....

....

....

....

....

Date: .... Day: ....

Today I am Grateful for

....

....

....

....

....

....

The wise man belongs
to all countries, for the
home of a great soul is
the whole world.

-Democritus

Date: .... Day: ....

Today I am Grateful for

....

....

....

....

....

Date: .... Day: ....

Today I am Grateful for

....

....

....

....

....

Date: .... Day: ....

Today I am Grateful for

....

....

....

....

....

....

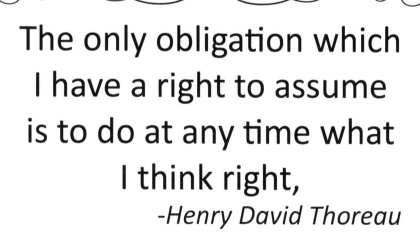

The only obligation which
I have a right to assume
is to do at any time what
I think right,
-Henry David Thoreau

Date: .... Day: ....

Today I am Grateful for

....

....

....

....

....

....

Date: .... Day: ....

Today I am Grateful for

....

....

....

....

....

When a thing ceases
to be a subject of
controversy, it ceasesto
be a subject of interest.
-William Hazlitt

Date: .... Day: ....

Today I am Grateful for

....

....

....

....

....

....

Date:............................ Day:..............................

Today I am Grateful for

....
....
....
....
....

Date:............................ Day:..............................

Today I am Grateful for

....
....
....
....
....

Date: .... Day: ....

Today I am Grateful for

....

....

....

....

....

....

Genius begins great
works; labor alone
finishes them.
-Joseph Joubert

Date:............................ Day:............................

Today I am Grateful for

....

....

....

....

....

Date:............................ Day:............................

Today I am Grateful for

....

....

....

....

....

The babe at first feeds upon
the mother's bosom,
but it is always on her heart.
-Henry Ward Beecher

Date:_____ Day:_____

Today I am Grateful for

....

....

....

....

....

....

Date: .... Day: ....

Today I am Grateful for

....

....

....

....

....

....

Date: .... Day: ....

Today I am Grateful for

....

....

....

....

....

Date:............................ Day:..................................

Today I am Grateful for

....

....

....

....

....

....

Nothing exists except atoms and empty space; everything else is opinion.

-*Democritus*

Date:............................ Day:..

Today I am Grateful for

....

....

....

....

....

Date:............................ Day:..

Today I am Grateful for

....

....

....

....

....

Date: .... Day: ....

Today I am Grateful for

....

....

....

....

....

....

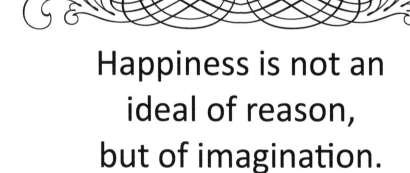

Happiness is not an
ideal of reason,
but of imagination.
-Immanuel Kant

Date: .... Day: ....

Today I am Grateful for

....

....

....

....

....

Date: .... Day: ....

Today I am Grateful for

....

....

....

....

....

By a lie, a man...
annihilates his dignity
as a man.
-Immanuel Kant

Date: .... Day: ....

Today I am Grateful for

....

....

....

....

....

....

Date: .... Day: ....

Today I am Grateful for

....

....

....

....

....

....

Date: .... Day: ....

Today I am Grateful for

....

....

....

....

....

....

Date: .... Day: ....

Today I am Grateful for

....

....

....

....

....

....

Grace has been defined
as the outward expression
of the inward harmony
of the soul.

-William Hazlitt

Date: .... Day: ....

Today I am Grateful for

....

....

....

....

....

Date: .... Day: ....

Today I am Grateful for

....

....

....

....

....

Love and fear. Everything
the father of a family says
must inspire one or
the other.

-Joseph Joubert

Date: .... Day: ....

Today I am Grateful for

....
....
....
....
....
....

47

Date: .... Day: ....

Today I am Grateful for

....

....

....

....

....

....

Date: .... Day: ....

Today I am Grateful for

....

....

....

....

....

Date: .... Day: ....

Today I am Grateful for

....

....

....

....

....

....

Two things awe me most,
the starry sky above me
and the moral law
within me.

-Immanuel Kant

Date:................................ Day:...

Today I am Grateful for

....

....

....

....

....

....

Date:................................ Day:...

Today I am Grateful for

....

....

....

....

....

Date: .... Day: ....

Today I am Grateful for

....

....

....

....

....

The question is not
what you look at,
but what you see..
-Henry David Thoreau

Date: .... Day: ....

Today I am Grateful for

....
....
....
....
....
....

Date: .... Day: ....

Today I am Grateful for

....
....
....
....
....

A part of kindness consists
in loving people more
than they deserve.

-Joseph Joubert

Date:.. Day:...

Today I am Grateful for

....

....

....

....

....

....

Date: .... Day: ....

Today I am Grateful for

....
....
....
....
....
....

Date: .... Day: ....

Today I am Grateful for

....
....
....
....
....

54

Date:_____ Day:_____

Today I am Grateful for

_____

_____

_____

_____

_____

_____

Gratitude is the fairest
blossom which springs
from the soul.
-Henry Ward Beecher

Date: _____ Day: _____

Today I am Grateful for

....

....

....

....

....

Date: _____ Day: _____

Today I am Grateful for

....

....

....

....

....

Live your life as though your
every act were to become
a universal law.

-Immanuel Kant

Date: .... Day: ....

Today I am Grateful for

....

....

....

....

....

....

Date: .... Day: ....

Today I am Grateful for

....

....

....

....

....

Date: .... Day: ....

Today I am Grateful for

....

....

....

....

....

Date: .... Day: ....

Today I am Grateful for

....

....

....

....

....

....

Everything existing in
the universe is the fruit
of chance and necessity.

-Democritus

Date: .... Day: ....

Today I am Grateful for

....

....

....

....

....

....

Date: .... Day: ....

Today I am Grateful for

....

....

....

....

....

Date: .... Day: ....

Today I am Grateful for

....

....

....

....

....

....

Politeness is the flower
of humanity.
                    -Joseph Joubert

Date:_____ Day:_____

Today I am Grateful for

....

....

....

....

....

Date:_____ Day:_____

Today I am Grateful for

....

....

....

....

....

Science is organized knowledge. Wisdom is organized life.

-Immanuel Kant

Date:............................. Day:...............................

Today I am Grateful for

....

....

....

....

....

....

Date: .... Day: ....

Today I am Grateful for

....

....

....

....

....

....

Date: .... Day: ....

Today I am Grateful for

....

....

....

....

....

....

Date: .... Day: ....

Today I am Grateful for

....

....

....

....

....

....

Rather than love,
than money, than fame,
give me truth.
-Henry Ward Beecher

Date: _____ Day: _____

Today I am Grateful for

....

....

....

....

....

....

Date: _____ Day: _____

Today I am Grateful for

....

....

....

....

....

....

It is better to debate a question without settling it than to settle a question without debating it.

-Joseph Joubert

Date: .... Day: ....

Today I am Grateful for

....

....

....

....

....

....

Date:_____ **Day:**_____

Today I am Grateful for

....

....

....

....

....

....

Date:_____ **Day:**_____

Today I am Grateful for

....

....

....

....

....

Date: .... Day: ....

Today I am Grateful for

....

....

....

....

....

....

Every charitable act
is a stepping stone
toward heaven.
-Henry Ward Beecher

Date:_____ Day:_____

Today I am Grateful for

....

....

....

....

....

Date:_____ Day:_____

Today I am Grateful for

....

....

....

....

....

Date: .... Day: ....

Today I am Grateful for

....

....

....

....

....

....

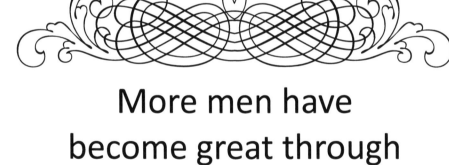

More men have
become great through
practice than by
nature.

-Democritus

Date:_____ Day:_____

Today I am Grateful for

....

....

....

....

....

....

Date:_____ Day:_____

Today I am Grateful for

....

....

....

....

....

....

Dreams are the touchstones of our characters.
-Henry David Thoreau

Date: .... Day: ....

Today I am Grateful for

....

....

....

....

....

....

Date: .... Day: ....

Today I am Grateful for

....

....

....

....

....

Date: .... Day: ....

Today I am Grateful for

....

....

....

....

....

Date: .... Day: ....

Today I am Grateful for

....

....

....

....

....

....

It is greed to do all
the talking but not to
want to listen at all.

-Democritus

Date:_____ Day:_____

Today I am Grateful for

....
....
....
....
....
....

Date:_____ Day:_____

Today I am Grateful for

....
....
....
....
....
....

Love is the river of life in the world.
-Henry Ward Beecher

Date: .... **Day:** ....

Today I am Grateful for

....

....

....

....

....

....

77

Date:.......................... Day:..........................

Today I am Grateful for

....

....

....

....

....

Date:.......................... Day:..........................

Today I am Grateful for

....

....

....

....

....

Date: .... Day: ....

Today I am Grateful for

....

....

....

....

....

....

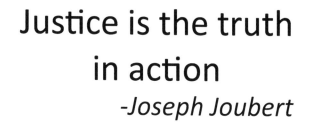

Justice is the truth
in action
-Joseph Joubert

Date: _____ Day: _____

Today I am Grateful for

....

....

....

....

....

Date: _____ Day: _____

Today I am Grateful for

....

....

....

....

....

Date: .... Day: ....

Today I am Grateful for

....

....

....

....

....

....

The animal needing
something knows how
much it needs, the
man does not.

-Democritus

Date:_____ Day:_____

Today I am Grateful for

....

....

....

....

....

....

Date:_____ Day:_____

Today I am Grateful for

....

....

....

....

....

Go confidently in the
direction of your dreams!
Live the life you've
imagined.
-Henry David Thoreau

Date: .... Day: ....

Today I am Grateful for

....

....

....

....

....

....

Date:............................ Day:............................

Today I am Grateful for

....

....

....

....

....

....

Date:............................ Day:............................

Today I am Grateful for

....

....

....

....

....

Date: .... Day: ....

Today I am Grateful for

....

....

....

....

....

....

I would rather sit on a
pumpkin, and have it all to
myself, than be crowded
on a velvet cushion.
-Henry David Thoreau

85

Date:............................ Day:......................................

Today I am Grateful for

....

....

....

....

....

Date:............................ Day:......................................

Today I am Grateful for

....

....

....

....

....

A person without a sense of humor is like a wagon without springs. It's jolted by every pebble on the road.

-Henry Ward Beecher

Date: .... Day: ....

Today I am Grateful for

....

....

....

....

....

....

87

Date:................................... Day:...

Today I am Grateful for

....

....

....

....

....

Date:................................... Day:...

Today I am Grateful for

....

....

....

....

....

Date: _____ Day: _____

Today I am Grateful for

....

....

....

....

....

....

Moderation multiplies pleasures, and increases pleasure.

-Democritus

Date:.......................... Day:...

Today I am Grateful for

....

....

....

....

....

....

Date:.......................... Day:...

Today I am Grateful for

....

....

....

....

....

Date: .... Day: ....

Today I am Grateful for

....

....

....

....

....

....

In law a man is guilty when he violates the rights of others. In ethics he is guilty if he only thinks of doing so.

-Immanuel Kant

91

Date: .... Day: ....

Today I am Grateful for

....

....

....

....

....

....

Date: .... Day: ....

Today I am Grateful for

....

....

....

....

....

The only vice that cannot be forgiven is hypocrisy. The repentance of a hypocrite is itself hypocrisy.

-William Hazlitt

Date: .... Day: ....

Today I am Grateful for

....

....

....

....

....

Date:............................ Day:..

Today I am Grateful for

....

....

....

....

....

....

Date:............................ Day:..

Today I am Grateful for

....

....

....

....

....

....

Date: .... Day: ....

Today I am Grateful for

....

....

....

....

....

....

Nothing makes the earth seem so spacious as to have friends at a distance; they make the latitudes and longitudes.

-Henry David Thoreau

95

Date: _____ Day: _____

Today I am Grateful for

....
....
....
....
....
....

Date: _____ Day: _____

Today I am Grateful for

....
....
....
....
....

96

A hypocrite despises those whom he deceives, but has no respect for himself. He would make a dupe of himself too, if he could.

-William Hazlitt

Date: _____ Day: _____

Today I am Grateful for

....

....

....

....

....

....

97

Date: .... Day: ....

Today I am Grateful for

....

....

....

....

....

....

Date: .... Day: ....

Today I am Grateful for

....

....

....

....

....

....

Date: .... Day: ....

Today I am Grateful for

....

....

....

....

....

....

We should not judge people
by their peak of excellence;
but by the distance they have
traveled from the point
where they started.

-Henry Ward Beecher

Date: .... Day: ....

Today I am Grateful for

....

....

....

....

....

Date: .... Day: ....

Today I am Grateful for

....

....

....

....

....

Top 10 memorable events in my life that I am Grateful for:

....

....

....

....

....

....

....

....

....

....

....

....

....

....

Top 10 places i have visited and I am Grateful for:

Notes

Made in the USA
Columbia, SC
12 June 2025

59315742R00065